Villa
d'E
STE

VILLA d'ESTE

a pictorial itinerary

De Luca Editori d'Arte

MINISTERO PER I BENI E LE ATTIVITÀ CULTURALI
SOPRINTENDENZA PER I BENI ARCHITETTONICI, PER IL PAESAGGIO
E PER IL PATRIMONIO STORICO ARTISTICO E DEMOETNOANTROPOLOGICO DEL LAZIO

Texts by MARIA LUISA MADONNA

Photographs by BEATRICE PEDICONI, GIANLUCA BIANCHI, NICO MARZIALI

Transalation by LUCINDA BYATT

Villa d'Este

Villa d'Este, a masterpiece of the Italian garden designated by Unesco as a world heritage site, with its terraces and impressive concentration of fountains, nymphaea, water jets and water-powered musical instruments, represents a much emulated model for European gardens of the Mannerist and Baroque periods. Thanks to the Villa d'Este, Tivoli itself has become synonymous with parks for collective recreation. Moreover, this *giardino delle meraviglie* must be seen against Tivoli's extraordinary landscape and its artistic and historical context: a few ruins from the ancient Tibur – like the Roman amphitheatre near the fifteenth-century fortress – are still visible among the throng of medieval churches and historic buildings. The archaeological ruins of numerous villas from the Republican and Imperial eras underline Tivoli's role as a site favoured by the Roman aristocracy and Emperors; such prestigious remains and evocative architecture add to the fascinating nature of the Tiburtine area, full of ravines, caves and waterfalls. The presence of travertine stone – the symbol of a millenary struggle between water and stone –, used since antiquity together with the rustic "tartari" or lime deposits to build nymphaea and artificial grottoes, is just one of the many elements that contributed to the conception of Villa d'Este. The arched construction of the central terrace and the Fountain of "Rometta" are visible from the countryside, blending into the overall view of the town together with the Temple of Hercules Triumphant. The imposing constructions and tiered terraces are reminiscent of the Hanging Gardens of Semiramis in Babylon, one of the seven wonders of the antique world. The project was almost demiurgic in nature, evoking the wonder of an epic and miraculous creation, to use the words of Daniele Barbaro: "in the works at Tivoli, it is fitting for nature to confess that it has been overcome by art and by the splendour of its soul. How otherwise would the gardens have been conceived in an instant, the woods grown and the trees filled with the sweetest fruits, the mountains appeared overnight having emerged from the valleys, and the iron-hard rocks of the mountains become beds for rivers, and the rock cleft to make way for water which has flooded the dry land, irrigated by fountains and running streams, and very rare fish-ponds" (from the dedication to Ippolito d'Este in Vitruvius's *Architettura*, 1567).

Cardinal Ippolito II d'Este (1509-72), son of Lucrezia Borgia and nephew of Pope Alexander VI, as well being related to King François I of France, revived the splendour of the courts at Ferrara, Rome and Fontainebleau at the Villa. Governor of Tivoli from 1550, he immediately cherished the idea of building a garden on the steep slope under the Palace, known as the "Valle Gaudente" and then filled with houses, churches, vineyards and woods. At the same time, he embarked on the programme of works to renew the traditional seat of the governors of Tivoli, already partly rebuilt in the early 16th century. But the project for a vast garden stretching from the Church of St. Peter and the medieval city walls, which acted as the Villa boundary, only became clear after 1560.

Within the framework of the "antiquarian" project for the Villa, Ippolito truly saw himself as an heir to those emperors, who had built villas in the Tiburtine area, and like Hadrian, he sought to reproduce in ideal terms a concentration of nearby and distant landscapes. From a closer analysis of Pirro Ligorio's antiquarian studies (we refer to both the manuscript volume in Turin dedicated to Tivoli and its classic villas, and to numerous other passages on the theme throughout his *Enciclopedia dell'Antichità*), it is clear that he was almost certainly the mind behind the architectural, antiquarian and iconological programme for the Villa; it is worth recalling that Ligorio had been commissioned as early as 1550 to undertake excavations and research at Hadrian's Villa. Working alongside Ligorio was the court architect, Giovanni Alberto Galvani, who was responsible for all the construction work.

Like the other Italian and French residences owned by this great nobleman, the prestigious villa became a rendezvous for literati, poets and musicians following the pattern of the classic "Academia" (one of these, the Frenchman Marcantonio Muret, defined Ippolito as "pater litterarum"). The villa also provided a setting for the ceremonial splendour of the Este family, which was enhanced by the decoration of the rooms, the costumes, the furnishings, the magnificence of the table and even the dishes. The rooms in the "Cardinal's Apartment" on the upper floor were decorated with a fitting ornamental display. From 1563 onwards, a host of painters, initially led by Girolamo Muziano and then by Livio Agresti and Federico Zuccari, started work on the rooms, which were almost completed by the cardinal's death (1572). The rooms were hung with Flemish tapestries and Spanish stamped leather, in gold and silver designs, and housed the Cardinal's fine collection of antique statues. This extraordinary wealth of antiquities and furnishings was lost and only the stuccoes and frescoes offer evidence of this former splendour. The decorative cycle was centred on a celebration of the cardinal, which accounts for the obsessive presence of the white eagle and fleurs-de-lys, the heraldic symbols of the Este family.

The decorations on the lower floor, to be used as a reception area, range from the sacred to the profane, focusing in particular on a celebration of the Este family and the legendary Tiburtine history; a constant theme is the "antiquarian" style and the use of architectural *trompe l'oeils* to enlarge the rooms.

In 1605 Cardinal Alessandro d'Este (1568-1624) embarked on a major renewal of the garden which, over the following decades, led to the construction of new fountains designed, among others, by Gianlorenzo Bernini. In the eighteenth century the Villa was abandoned for many years and its antiquarian furnishings were dispersed to museums throughout Europe. In 1803 the property was inherited by the Habsburgs and then in 1851 by Cardinal Gustav von Hohenlohe (1823-1896), who gave a Christian interpretation to some of the fountains in the garden.

During the First World War, Villa d'Este became state property, thus ending the long period of abandonment (apart from the Hohenlohe interval), plundering and degeneration. Between the Wars, the Villa was revived by the loving restoration work directed by Attilio Rossi; over the past twenty years, much of the Palace and the garden has been the focus of a scientific restoration campaign led by Isabella Barisi, which is still underway.

Aerial view of the garden of Villa d'Este with the Fishponds and the Water Organ (Photo Kamera Studio di Aldo Ippoliti for Sara Nistri) ▶

◄ The Palace courtyard with the Fountain of Venus and, in the background, the church of S. Maria Maggiore.

The loggia in the courtyard. At the back, on the right, is the entrance to the Cardinal's Apartment.

The courtyard is surrounded by a portico on three sides, while the fourth backs onto the church. The space is dominated by the Fountain of Venus (1568-69), an allusion to Nature generatrix and universal love. The antique statue, reclining and asleep, evokes the symbolic slumber that reveals the secrets of the garden; behind her is an ideal representation of the waters flowing across the Tiburtine landscape; around her, branches of golden apples hint at the Garden of the Hesperides.

The Salone on the upper floor
below: The coat of arms of Cardinal
Ippolito d'Este on the ceiling of the
Antechamber.

The view from the Salone overlooks the
gardens and the wide panorama beyond.

The decoration (started in the spring of
1568 under the supervision of Livio
Agresti) is limited to the frieze and the
vaulted ceiling. The largest ceiling panels and the ovals of the frieze are unfinished. The allegorical ensemble is a
celebration of Ippolito's moral qualities,
and his presence is recalled by the stucco coats of arms in the corners of the
room. The frieze depicts a sequence of
twenty *Virtues*, alternated with oval
stucco frames that would have contained the portraits or deeds of illustri-
ous figures. The four panels on the
longer sides of the vaulted ceiling contain landscapes inspired by the Tiburtine landscape (the temples of Hercules
and the Sibyl, bridges, ruins and rivers);
on the shorter sides are the *Four Seasons* in small ovals surrounded by
grotesque decoration. The unfinished
works in the centre of the ceiling are
framed by a frieze made from garlands
of flowers, fruit and vegetables with
fleurs-de-lys and the Este eagles.

Views with landscapes inspired by Tivoli in the vaulted ceiling of the Salone on the upper floor.

The Chapel of Cardinal Ippolito. ▶

The Chapel was frescoed in 1572 by Federico Zuccari and others. On its walls are frescoes of the *Prophets* and two Sibyls; in the centre of the barrel vault is the *Coronation of the Virgin* and, above the altar, *God the Father in glory with music-making angels*. The fresco above the altar is much later and is a copy of the famous *Madonna della Ghiara*.

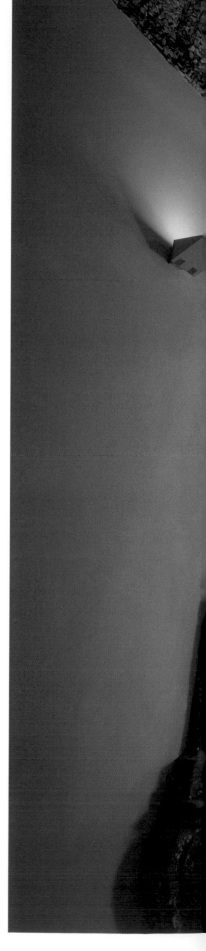

Ceiling of the cryptoporticus or "manica lunga". (Photo M. Benedetti, S.B.A.P.P.S.A.D. Lazio)

The long corridor connecting the rooms on the ground floor is built in the fashion of a Roman cryptoporticus, with light entering from the courtyard above. The initial stretch of the barrel vault, closest to the staircase, is decorated with mosaic: recent restoration work has renewed the pergola with its floral motifs and different bird species; a larger panel depicts a winged figure with a trumpet.

Three rustic Fountains are set opposite the doors into the Rooms (two were installed in 1569 by Ludovico de Negri and the fountain designer Andrea Romano, and the third was finished a few years later) to delight the cardinal's guests with the sound of water. Each fountain has a niche with an apsidal shell-shaped basin containing rocks made from lime deposit and a deep pool; the decorations include plaster bas-relief and rich mosaics in glass tesserae, polychrome enamels and mixed stones; the recurrent motif depicting the boughs of apples from the Gardens of Hesperides and the eagles allude to the source of patronage.

Room of the Fountain.

The main Salon (decorated at various intervals from 1565 onwards, initially under the supervision of Girolamo Muziano) was used for the cardinal's banquets.

The "solomonic" (spiral) columns around the walls (inspired by those in St. Peter's) simulate an open loggia through which the landscape is visible; the wide perspective views mainly portray the Tiburtine countryside and the cardinal's magnificent residences: Villa d'Este, with the Water Organ and the Oval Fountain, and the villa on the Quirinal.

The lower part of the vault is embellished with delicate grotesque decorations in an antiquarian style; at the centre of each of the four sides, stucco frames contain scenes of *Sacrifices in honour of Apollo, Diana, Ceres and Bacchus*, perhaps alluding to the seasons and centred on colossal heads. *Jupiter, Juno, Neptune and Pluto* appear in four oval frames; lastly, in the corners of the vault, paired deities uphold the Este eagle. In the central rectangle (surrounded by an illusionistic loggia that may be the work of the Sienese painter Matteo Nerone) is the *Feast of the Gods*, inspired by the similar fresco of the *Wedding Feast* by Raphael in the Villa Farnesina.

The rustic fountain designed by the fountain expert Curzio Maccarone (finished in 1568 by Paolo Calandrino and embellished by Tivolino in 1570) transforms the Salone into an artificial garden and creates a link to the real garden.

on following pages:
The Feast of the Gods on the ceiling of the Room of the Fountain.

Views of the garden from the Room of the Fountain. Above, general view showing condition of the Villa in 1568; below, Water Organ (the fresco was repainted to show the water jets installed after 1925)

The rustic Fountain in the Salone. ▶

Clad in mosaic and polychrome enamels, the Fountain (designed by Maccarone, who also created a similar work in the Salone at Caprarola) is framed by two caryatids; the mosaic landscape with the Temple of the Sibyl portrays Tivoli in antiquity.

First Tiburtine Room: full view and vaulted ceiling.

Around the walls (frescoed in 1568-69), an illusionistic colonnade contains episodes showing the legendary origins of Tivoli inside mock tapestries. Special emphasis is given to the scene depicting *Hercules Saxanus* kneeling in front of his enemies, the protector of Tivoli as well as the Este family. Further up are small panels containing views of the Tiburtine countryside and even the Villa d'Este (the Oval Fountain still under construction can seen to the left of the window). The antecedent is portrayed in the centre of the ceiling, the *Landing of the three Greek brothers Catillus, Coras and Tiburtus in Latium and the battle against the Latini*; to the sides are four scenes showing the foundations of Tivoli: *The sacrifice made by the three brothers; The sacrifice for the foundation of Tibur, The construction of the walls, The construction of the first houses.*

20

Second Tiburtine Room.

As the pendant to the First Tiburtine Room, the fresco cycle completes the story of the origins of Tivoli, focusing in particular on the Sibyl Albunea or Tiburtine Sibyl.

The central theme tells the story of the metamorphosis of this mythical figure. Ino, wife of Athamas, wished to take care of Bacchus, the product of Jupiter's love for Semele, but she provoked Juno's anger who took revenge by turning Athamas mad and making him kill his son Clearchus. Ino fled with her other son Melicertes, saving herself with the help of Venus and Neptune who transformed them into the water deities Leucothea and Palaemon. Having landed in Italy, Ino-Leucothea became the first Mater Matuta (and her son Portunus, the god of ports) and then the Sibyl.

In the two oval panels on the ceiling, we see the *Madness of Athamas*, dashing his son Clearchus against a rock, and the *Drowning of King Anio in the river*; the two rectangular frames show *Ino as Mater Matuta and the river Tiber*, and opposite, *The Tiber, Aniene and Ercolaneo rivers*. The four ovals portray female figures with musical and theatrical attributes. In the centre of the vault, between the band of the zodiac, is the quadriga of *Apollo the Sun-god* drawn by four horses led by the genii of the day.

On the walls, embellished by an illusionistic architecture of columns and marble incrustations, the two large panels depict the *Sacrifice of the ram to the Mater Matuta* and the *Adoration of the Mater Matuta with her young son Portunus*; to the sides are the cardinal virtues, *Fortitude, Justice, Prudence and Temperance*. Beside the windows are panels containing landscapes and on the opposite side, a mock tapestry portraying *Venus and Neptune*, who saved Ino-Leucothea.

A section of the Roman villa dating from 1st century BC is visible below the floor. It was discovered during restoration work in 1987 and the floor mosaics date from 1st century AC.

◀ Frescoes on the vaulted ceiling of the Second Tiburtine Room.
Above: Adoration of the Mater Matuta or Tiburtine Sibyl. Below: The Aniene River and the Tiburtine Sibyl.
Hercules welcomed to Olympus on the ceiling of the Room of Hercules (Photo Giagnoli, S.B.A.P.P.S.A.D. Lazio)

The frescoes in the Room of Hercules were completed in 1565-66 by Girolamo Muziano and his assistants, and were the first to be carried out in the Palace.
The lower part of the ceiling portrays the *Twelve Feats of Hercules*: taken from Giovanni Boccaccio's *Genealogia deorum*, they represent the famous tasks that Hercules had to perform to be accepted among the Gods. One "feat" is depicted in an oval panel on each wall, flanked by a further two "feats" against a background of grotesque decoration. In the corners are the cardinal's stucco coats of arms surmounted by mixtilinear frames showing the *Cardinal Virtues*.
The epilogue of the myth, the *Apotheosis of Hercules* fills the centre of the vault: the hero, welcomed to the concourse of gods on Olympus is seen from behind, with the skin of the Nemean Lion on his back and his arms resting on his club.
The reference to Hercules, the conqueror of the golden apples of the Hesperides, provides a strong and constant element in the iconography of the Villa and its garden.

Room of Nobility.

The frescoed decorations of this room and the successive Room of Glory (completed by Federico Zuccari and his assistants in 1566-67) celebrate the moral qualities of Cardinal Ippolito.

The architectural illusion of the columns and polychrome marble incrustations frames the allegories of the *Virtues* and *Liberal Arts* against a "Pompeian red" background in antiquarian style; the mock busts portray philosophers and legislators of antiquity: *Plato, Pythagorus, Bias, Solon, Diogenes, Socrates* and *Periander*.

Grotesque decoration surrounds the allegories of *Honour, Rerum Natura, Opulence* and *Immortality* on the ceiling. In the centre *Nobility* is enthroned under an aerial canopy, flanked by her handmaids *Liberality* and *Generosity*. In the corners, the *impresa* of Cardinal Ippolito with the white eagle, two boughs of golden apples and the motto *Ab insomni non custodita dracone,* an allusion to Hercules's eleventh feat.

Apotheosis of the Nobility, centre of the ceiling in the Room of Nobility
Room of Glory. ▶

Frescoed in 1566-68 by Federico Zuccari and his assistants (and possibly repainted at a later date) the decoration in the Room of Glory is based on a combination of numerous figurative elements.
Using a recurrent motif in 15ᵗʰ-century painting, two shelved cupboards are painted illusionistically on the walls. Their curtains are partially drawn aside to display the contents. This device is used to represent items linked to Cardinal Ippolito, including his cardinal's hat and the papal tiara.
Between the mock classical busts on the walls, generous drapes open to reveal the frames containing the four cardinal virtues: *Justice*, *Fortitude*, *Prudence* and *Temperance*.
The vaulted ceiling exalts the virtues that enable the attainment of *Glory* (frescoed in the central panel, and now lost); the allegories of *Magnanimity*, *Fortune*, *Time* and *Religion* are depicted in oval and octagonal stucco frames.

Allegory of the
Fountain on the
ceiling of the
Room of Glory;
note the cardinal's
hat and the papal
tiara falling out of
the sky, an allusion
to Ippolito d'Este's
ecclesiastical
ambitions.

Allegory of
Temperance on a
wall in the Room
of Glory .

Room of the Hunt.

This is the only room frescoed after Ippolito's death (traditionally attributed to Antonio Tempesta, the frescoes are more probably the work of an unknown landscape painter from the early 17th century).
The hunting scenes in the woods and rivers depicted in the large panels are alternated with hunting trophies (boar, buck, hare, game birds) and garlands of flowers and fruit; other smaller landscapes are painted in the window and door embrasures. Among the other scenes it is worth mentioning the sea battles, shipwrecks and even a fire, which introduces the fourth element, fire, to counter the preponderance of earth, air and water.

on following page:
Details of the Room of the Hunt with various hunting trophies and hunting scenes.

The garden

The first plots of land were purchased in 1550 during a vast campaign of expropriations involving the houses and land in the "Valle Gaudente", but work on the garden only began after 1560. Water to supply the main fountains was taken directly from the Aniene river through a 200-metre-long underground conduit dug in 1564-65; the other fountains were fed by the Rivellese aqueduct begun in 1560. As was stated earlier, Pirro Ligorio was undoubtedly the brain behind the garden and until 1569 he worked alongside the Cardinal's favourite architect, Gian Alberto Galvani.

The "impresa" of Cardinal Ippolito – the eagle grasping a bough of golden apples, with the motto from Ovid "Ab insomni non custodita dracone" – alludes to Hercules's victory over the dragon Ladon in the garden of the Hesperides containing the tree of golden apples. The following Latin verses were dedicated by the humanist Muret to his friend Ippolito: "The golden apples, which Hercules stole from the sleeping Dragon, are now owned by Ippolito. As a token of his gratefulness, Ippolito wishes to dedicate the gardens planted here to the author of the gift". Villa d'Este was therefore conceived as the Garden of the Hesperides dedicated to Hercules, the mythical ancestor of the Este family.

To this heraldic-topographical interpretation, we should also add the presence of a series of important female divinities, almost in the role of *great mothers*, from Ino-Leucothea (or Mater Matuta or the Sibyl Albunea) to Venus and the "Nature Goddess" (Diana of Ephesus), which represent the most revealing and secret spirit of the Villa, namely the idea of *Nature generatrix*. The figure of Venus Generatrix is important in this sense, sleeping like a *nympha loci* and placed in the Fountain in the courtyard which cryptographically concludes the central axis of the garden, apparently dominated by numerous statues of Hercules.

With its complex spatial layout, the theatrical importance of its architecture and the antiquarian influence of its decorative theme, the garden was conceived as a microcosm that metaphorically recreated the Tiburtine countryside: "there is in fact a hidden explanation, not lacking elegance, namely to restore nature to the Tiburtine ground as conceived by that famous architect of our time and my great friend, Pirro Ligorio, a man of extraordinary and wide-ranging erudition, renowned for his wonderful knowledge of all antiquity" (U. Foglietta, 1569).

The largest fountains are genuine "teatri d'acqua", models that were copied over and over again in later years. The exceptional blend of architecture that emulates the antique, marvellous devices (like the water organs), a wide variety of tree species, but above all water displays of unprecedented beauty were described by one contemporary as follows: "the gushing water creates... marvellous effects ... not only do you see numerous beautiful waterfalls in various shapes, but you hear them produce feigned artillery shots and fake birds can be seen appearing and disappearing around an owl, singing and making natural gestures; from the same fountain you even hear the sound of musical organs being played, an effect that is certainly supernatural" (G. Saminiati, c. 1580). The luxuriant growth of the trees now makes it difficult to see the geometric design of the villa from a distance or from above.

The double loggia of the Palace and view overlooking the garden.

The two-storey loggia with Palladian windows (1566-68), flanked by two stairs, was inspired by Michelangelo's designs for Campidoglio and the lower part contains the small grotto of Leda.
From here there is a magnificent view of the garden (the central axis is dominated by the Fountain of the Dragons and the Cypress Circle) and the surrounding countryside and hills from the loggias and the balcony surrounding the Fountain of the Tripod.

The Grotto of Diana. In the foreground, on the left, is Daphne's metamorphosis into a laurel. Below: an oval on the ceiling portraying Perseus and Andromeda.

The cruciform nymphaeum (constructed in 1570-72, by Lola and Paolo Calandrino from Bologna whose names are inscribed on scrolls on the pedestals of the caryatids beside the statue of Diana the huntress) has been completely stripped of all its antique statues, and the large stucco reliefs covered with mosaic have deteriorated; the other polychrome mosaics made from various materials have fared better.

The Grotto is dedicated to Diana, the goddess of hunting who was given eternal virginity by her father Jupiter, becoming a symbol of chastity. In addition to statues and mosaics of heroines like *Lucretia* and the *Amazon Penthesileia* who chose chastity, the grotto is dominated by large bas-reliefs with scenes inspired by Ovid's Metamorphoses, depicting the tragic stories of heroines, like the nymphs *Daphne* and *Syrinx*, who, finding themselves pursued by Apollo and Pan, prayed for a metamorphosis to protect their purity and were transformed respectively into a laurel tree and reed; we also see *Callisto*, Diana's nymph, who was transformed into a she-bear as punishment for having violated her vow of chastity during her affair with Jupiter.

Close-up of the Grotto of Diana. At the top you can see the floor tiles painted with the Este fleur-de-lys and dated "1572".

The entrance to the Grotto leads into a rectangular vestibule with a cross-vault; the lunettes are emphasised by spirals of entwined boughs bearing the golden apples of the Hesperides and are decorated with floral motifs, horns of plenty and Este fleurs-de-lys; the oval frames depict *Perseus and Andromeda* and *Jupiter carrying off Europa*.

The main room also has a cross-vault; four pairs of caryatids on pedestals at the four corners carry baskets of fruit on their heads; branches of golden apples grow up over the vault, culminating in the Este eagle in the centre. On the end wall, a large semicircular niche with the rustic fountain originally housed an antique statue of *Diana*.

Two rectangular side rooms with barrel vaults are decorated with reliefs portraying scenes from the *Metamorphoses*. The room on the left has another rustic fountain which originally contained a statue of *Minerva*; on the right, a large arch opens into a covered loggia, overlooking the Tiburtine countryside and embellished with mythological scenes and mosaic grotesque decoration.

The sixteenth-century coloured floor tiles, some of which are still conserved at the back of the nymphaeum, contain the heraldic motifs of Cardinal Ippolito and were made in 1572 by the master ceramist Bernardino de' Gentili di Aversa.

The Tivoli or Oval Fountain.

The Tivoli Fountain, also known as the Oval Fountain is always described as the most magnificent "teatro d'acqua" in the villa. It was constructed by Curzio Maccarone in 1564-70 to a design by Pirro Ligorio. A wide arched exedra rises behind the large oval basin and the niches between the arches contained ten *Nymphs* in peperino holding vases from which water shot into the basin. Fan-shaped sprays also spurted from vases under the arches; the spectacular cascade flowed over the large bowl, out of which jets of water rose to form the outline of a fleur-de-lys.

An artificially porous hill rises above the exedra, which originally oozed water through a system of terracotta slits hidden in clefts of rock; the hill contains three grottoes out of which water pours into three vases placed below the colossal statues of the *Mater Matuta or Tiburtine Sibyl* (or Ino Leucothea, the protagonist of the metamorphosis portrayed in the frescoes of the Second Tiburtine Room) and the river-gods *Ercolaneo* and *Aniene*. The Tivoli Fountain forms part of a complex iconological programme conceived by Pirro Ligorio which includes the Hundred Fountain walk and the "Rometta" Fountain. The system is a metaphorical allusion to the physical nature of the surrounding terrain, showing the Tiburtine mountain, the artificially reconstructed caverns and the rivers.

At the top of the artificial mountain is a representation of the mythical winged horse Pegasus landing on Mount Parnassus. Where his hoof stamped the rock, the Hippocrene spring flowed out of the ground and nourished the Muses who inspired the Arts. The Tiburtine mountain was assimilated to Parnassus: thanks to the protection and artistic patronage of Cardinal Ippolito d'Este, the waters of Tivoli also flowed and the arts flourished.

Two small niches on the wall opposite the Fountain (built in 1569) contained two statues of *Bacchus* in peperino (these were replaced by the actual stucco versions in the 17th century). Their presence is linked to the myth of Ino Leucothea, Bacchus's foster-mother.

The Grotto of Venus, later known as the Grotto of Bacchus, also opens into this enclosure. The following is a contemporary description: "a marble statue of Venus, in full relief, stands naked and very beautiful... at her feet is a shell out of which rises a jet of water so the room is pleasurably cool in summer and the sound of the bubbling water creates various effects" *(G. M. Zappi, 1576).*

Oval Fountain. The portico behind
the waterfall.

The Hundred Fountains.

The long walk joins the Fountain of Tivoli with the Fountain of Rome and is flanked by three channels terraced one above the other, creating a dramatic sequence of fountains (the work, originally designed by Pirro Ligorio, was built between 1565 and 1571). The fountain represents the antique course followed by the Tiburtine rivers, the Albuneo, the Ercolaneo and the Aniene.

There were originally twenty-two boats along the upper channel; the fleurs-de-lys and eagles were added in 1622, and the obelisks later still. At the back of the central channel were stucco panels showing scenes from Ovid's *Metamorphoses;* along the back of the lower channel, between the jets of water spouting from the mouths of animal masks, was a sequence of mosaic sea-monsters.

Spreading mosses and limestone deposits have almost completely covered and partly worn away the fine decorations.

on following pages:
The "Rometta" Fountain with the ruins of Rome's monuments, the Tiburtine mountain, the statue of Tiber and the boat-shaped Isola Tiberina with obelisk.

◀ The statues on the Fountain of Rome or "Rometta", with the city of Rome in the distance.
The Mountain of the Aniene with the statues of Apennines (centre) and Tiber (right).

The "Rometta" Fountain (erected by Curzio Maccarone in 1567-70 to a design by Pirro Ligorio) brings to an end the symbolic itinerary conceived by Ligorio: the waters of the rivers rising from Monte Tiburtino (Fontain of Tivoli) flow down to meet the Tiber at the gates of Rome, represented by the theatrical backdrop of the "Rometta" fountain which faces the Eternal city. From left to right, the metaphor starts with the artificial hill (added in the early seventeenth century) and waterfall over the river-god *Aniene*; another grotto houses the personification of the *Apennines;* below, the Aniene flows into the Tiber, symbolised by the marble statue in the right-hand grotto. From here, the waters flow towards the stone boat with an obelisk that represents the Isola Tiberina. A series of small buildings symbolising the hills of Rome and its key monuments stood in a semicircle around the fountain, but most have been lost. On the edge of the terrace, in line with the Tiburtine Sibyl in the Oval Fountain opposite, you can still see the statue of *Rome Victorious* by the Fleming Pierre de la Motte (1568) and the *Wolf suckling the twins* (by the same artist).

Fountain of the Emperors or Proserpina.

The Fountain (built by Alberto Galvani in 1569-70) should have contained the statues of the Roman Emperors, like Hadrian, who built villas in the Tiburtine territory. In the form of a triumphal arch, the elevation contains "Solomonic" columns inspired by those in St. Peter's. The sculptural group of *Pluto carrying off Proserpina* was inserted in 1640 above a large shell supported by two horses.

Fountain of the Owl. ▶

The triumphal arch is framed by two columns with mosaics depicting boughs of golden apples; the attic carries the cardinal's shield topped by the Este eagle and fleurs-de-lys.
Recent restoration work (project by L. Lombardi; construction by R. Briscoe with profiles painted by E. Farina) has renewed the hydraulic mechanism created by Leclerc (1565-69) which copied an ancient invention from Alexandria: about twenty small metal birds on two bronze olive branches sang in different ways until silenced by the appearance of an owl.

Fountain of the Dragons.

In the original project the fountain was dominated by Ladon the hundred-headed Dragon who guarded the garden of the Hesperides from which Hercules stole the golden apples; the creation of four dragons is an allusion to the coat of arms of Pope Gregory XIII who visited the villa in 1572.

The spectacular water display from the large basin was renowned for its resounding sonorous effects (unfortunately now lost) caused by a complex system that altered the water pressure: "on occasions the water is made to sound like explosions from a small mortar or several arquebuses fired together; at other times, it spreads to form a tent-like shape, representing heavy rain" (A. Del Re, 1611). Two rivulets flow around the upper edge of the exedra enclosing the Fountain and fall into a sequence of shells.

The fish-ponds and the Fountain of Neptune.

Bernini constructed a naturalistic waterfall under the Water Organ in 1661, now almost completely lost. The restoration work undertaken by Attilio Rossi in 1927 led to the creation of the new Fountain of Neptune with its famous water display: the "twelve jets, placed to form a stepped display", are particularly evocative since they "bring to mind the hydraulic organ". The niche behind the curtain of water forms a monumental setting for the colossal unfinished torso of Neptune, which should have formed the centrepiece of the unbuilt Fountain of the Sea imagined by Ligorio beyond the fish-ponds.

The Water Organ.

Commenced in 1568 to a design by Ligorio, the Fountain is famous for its hydraulic organ, the first fully automatic model built in modern times (the work of French fountain experts Luc Leclerc and Claude Venard): it consisted of an airtight "aeolian chamber" to separate air from water; the water flow activated a hydraulic wheel which controlled the valves on the organ pipes, whereas air was ducted through lead pipes to the *sommier* and then distributed to the organ pipes.

The large central niche in the triumphal arch originally housed the statue of the *Ephesian Diana* or "*Mother Nature*". In the early 17th century the rocks were dismantled and an octagonal *tempietto* was erected with a double cupola. The mixtilinear basin at the base of the monumental "teatro d'acqua", contains the elegant, small balustraded terrace.

The organ was irremediably lost in the late 18th century, having been first damaged a few years after construction and on various other occasions. It has now been restored using a similar pneumo-hydraulic function (project by L. Lombardi, P. Barbieri, A. Latanza; installed by R. Briscoe).

Close-ups of the Water Organ: the double cupola of the tempietto, bas-relief with Orpheus and close-up of the statue of Apollo.

These form part of the works commissioned by Cardinal Alessandro d'Este (1568-1624), together with the creation of the tempietto, the pictorial decorations, the statues of *Apollo* and *Orpheus* and the bas-reliefs depicting the *Musical contest between Apollo and Marsyas* and *Orpheus taming the animals.*

View of the Cypress Circle today (only two majestic cypresses planted in the 17ᵗʰ century still survive).

Fountain of the "Nature Goddess" or Ephesian Diana (the statue, carved in 1568 by Gillis Van de Vliete to a design by Pirro Ligorio, was moved here in 1612 from the Water Organ). ▶

on following page:
The Fountain of the Dragons seen from the Stairs of the Bubbling Fountains.

Printed in Italy
by Tipar s.r.l., Rome

ISBN 88-8016-550-X